Genre Realistic F

 **Essential Question**
What can our connections to the world teach us?

by **Marie Langley**   illustrated by **Victor Kennedy**

Chapter 1

Always Said We Would

Tane

Tane's stomach felt strange. He was on an airplane that was flying above American Samoa. The airplane was descending toward the airport to land. The descent was not the only reason Tane felt strange.

Tane's dad, Sione, was from American Samoa. Sione had promised that the family would visit American Samoa someday. Now Tane and his family were getting ready to land on the Samoan island of Tutuila.

Tane had heard a lot about Tutuila, but this was his first visit to the island. Tane felt nervous and excited about meeting his grandparents and relatives for the first time.

Tane's dad had grown up on Tutuila.

Sione often told his children Tane and Tane's sister, Marama, stories about his life. "I was a good football player in high school. I won a football scholarship to go to college in the United States. Unfortunately, I got injured and couldn't play football anymore, but I finished school and earned a business degree. Then I got a job."

Sione also told his children about meeting his wife, Ruth, and getting married. Later, they had a daughter, Marama, and a son, Tane. Now Sione had his own business. It was successful. Finally, he could take his family to his homeland of Samoa.

Tane's father had always said to his children, "Wait until you see Tutuila and discover what life is like in a Samoan village."

Now as the airplane landed at the Pago Pago airport, Tane would finally experience island life.

As the family entered the airport terminal building, Marama said to Tane, "Look who's here!" Uncle Manu and Auntie Tiresa were waving and calling out to the family as they pushed through the crowd.

"*Talofa!*" Uncle Manu's voice blared across the arrival area. "Welcome home, brother. Welcome, all of you!" Uncle Manu embraced Tane tightly. Tane could barely breathe!

Tane's dad and Uncle Manu looked a lot alike. Tane had met his uncle and auntie two years ago when they had visited Tane's family in California.

Auntie Tiresa hugged Tane, too. She examined Tane from head to toe. She exclaimed, "Tane, you've grown so tall and handsome! It's wonderful to see you!" Auntie Tiresa hugged Tane and his family again.

Sione

Ruth

Auntie Tiresa

Uncle Manu helped Tane's family with the luggage. Uncle Manu said, "We rented a car for you, so you can drive to the village whenever you want."

"We'll see the rest of the family on the weekend. They are expecting to see you," Auntie Tiresa said.

Sione drove from the airport to Pago Pago. Tane and Marama commented excitedly about the people, stores, and buildings they saw during the trip.

Sione shook his head and said, "Look at all the stores and restaurants! And all the cars and trucks! I hope the village hasn't changed much."

STOP AND CHECK

Why is Tane's family going to Tutuila?

Chapter 2

Island Time

There was an enormous reception at the village. A large crowd of unfamiliar faces and sounds greeted Tane's family when they arrived.

Tane felt overwhelmed. Everyone wanted to shake Tane's hand, slap him on the back, or hug him. He couldn't remember the names of everyone he met.

Sione put an arm around Tane's shoulders and led him toward an older couple. Tane immediately knew who they were. "Say hello to your grandparents, son."

Tane stared at his grandparents. Tane had heard so much about them, and finally he was meeting them face to face. It seemed like a dream.

Tane said, "It's good to see you, Grandma and Grandpa."

"It's lovely to see you, too, Tane." Grandma smiled and pulled Tane close to her. "You look so much like your father when he was your age."

Grandpa didn't say anything. He seemed as overwhelmed with emotion as Tane was.

Grandpa

In Other Words in person. En español, *face to face* quiere decir *cara a cara*.

village

relatives

7

Soon Tane began to recognize his relatives. He met his father's two sisters and older brother. There were a lot of new cousins too!

Tane said to his sister, "Have you noticed those two girls? They look a lot like you."

Marama replied, "Listen to that boy over there. He sounds just like you! He even laughs like you. It's crazy! Suddenly we are part of a huge family!"

At first, Tane felt shy with his cousins, so he let Marama do most of the talking. When the cousins asked about America, Tane described his home. Soon he began to relax.

Tane and Marama learned that most of the villagers lived in traditional *fale*-style buildings. After the family had met everyone, Sione took Ruth, Marama, and Tane to show them his parents' home.

fale

palm fronds

roof

floor

Tane's grandparents lived in an oval-shaped fale. The roof was made of palm fronds, which rested on tall wooden poles. Woven mats covered the raised floor.

"Where are the walls?" Tane asked. He was confused.

Sione laughed and pointed to mats below the roof. They were rolled up and tied. Sione explained, "You can unroll the mats if you want privacy, but usually the mats stay rolled up. It's cooler that way."

"Where's the bedroom?" Marama asked. Sione pointed to a neat pile of bedding and sleeping mats.

"What about the kitchen?" Tane's mom asked.

"Everyone cooks in the *umukuka*, or cookhouse. It's at the back of the village," Sione replied.

"So there's no electricity in a fale?" Marama asked.

"That's right," Sione said.

Language Detective	Below the roof is a prepositional phrase. What noun does it describe?

9

Tane felt nervous again. He asked quietly, "Will we be sleeping in a fale, Dad?"

Sione looked at his son and said, "Why? Would you like to?"

"Um, I … I'm not sure," Tane stammered.

"Me neither. There's not much privacy," Tane's mom said.

Sione laughed, "I told you island life is different!"

"I could get used to it. It'll be like going camping," Marama said.

Tane's dad told the family, "I'm sure we'll get used to it. We'll stay at a hotel tonight and I'll do some errands. Then starting from tomorrow we'll stay here. Our time here is precious. I want us to spend as much time as we can with our family."

Tane could not relax that night. Starting tomorrow, he would have to stay in a house without walls and with people he hardly knew.

STOP AND CHECK

Describe the grandparents' house.

mats

bedding

Chapter 3

Even Closer

The next morning, everyone woke up early. At breakfast, Sione said, "We'll drive to the village after we run some errands."

When the family arrived at the village, Marama jumped out of the car and eagerly left to join her cousins. Sione and Ruth got out of the car, too, but Tane stayed in the car.

Tane said, "I don't feel well. I'll just sit here for a while."

His mom looked worried and asked, "Are you okay, Tane? Do you want me to stay with you?"

His father said, "Tane just needs some time. Come on. The others are expecting us."

Tane stared toward the ocean and tried not to cry. Why was it difficult to spend time with his family?

Just then, the car door opened, and Tane's grandmother climbed into the car next to him.

In Other Words at that moment. En español, *just then* quiere decir *en ese momento*.

Grandma looked around the car. She said, "Nice car. Is this why you don't want to get out?"

Tane shook his head and smiled a little.

Grandma took Tane's hand and squeezed it. She said, "You can't stay in the car forever, Tane. You have traveled a long way, and it has taken many years for you to be able to visit us. We are your family, and we have a special connection. This place is your home, too."

Tane swallowed hard. He wanted to cry.

Grandma smiled and said, "Besides, you'll cook like a fish on the fire if you stay in this hot car all day!"

Tane laughed. He knew Grandma was right.

backseat

Marama yelled to her brother, "Come on, Tane! The cousins are waiting for us at the lagoon. Hurry up!"

Grandma and Tane got out of the car. Then Tane ran after Marama to the beach. The cousins were playing in the lagoon. The sunlight danced on the water, and Tane dived into the sparkling waves. The water was wonderfully warm, and he forgot all his worries.

After the swim, Marama and Tane helped in the village garden. Then they helped to catch fish. Grandma cooked the fish in the umukuka. Tane thought it was the best fish he had ever tasted. Later, Tane remembered that his family would stay in the fale. He had never shared a room with so many people before. He laid down on a sleeping mat next to his parents. The sleeping mat felt surprisingly comfortable. A light breeze passed through the fale. In the distance, Tane heard waves on the sand.

Tane slept deeply, and he did not wake up until the sun was shining brightly and the roosters were crowing.

The days passed quickly. Tane enjoyed being part of a big family. Soon Tane could name all his aunts, uncles, and cousins.

Tane took photographs of everyone. One photo showed Tane with his best buddies, Sefa and Malaki. They were playing ball on the *malae*, the big grassy area in front of the village. In another photo, his cousins Pika, Lanuola, and Sina were teaching Marama to dance the *siva*. And another photograph showed Marama teaching the cousins dance moves she knew in exchange.

Tane took photographs of the grownups too. He took a photograph of Grandma, Auntie Tiresa, and Tane's mom weaving mats. Then Tane took a video of his dad and Uncle Manu racing canoes in the lagoon. The two brothers tried to tip over each other's canoes, laughing the entire time.

Sometimes, Sione sat <u>with Grandpa</u> and the other village elders in the *fale tele*, or council house. Tane did not know what they were discussing until the very last day of his family's visit.

Language Detective With Grandpa is a prepositional phrase. What verb does it describe?

The malae was crowded with family and friends sharing a final meal. Sione said, "I want you to know that it has been very important to bring my wife and children to meet all of you."

Sione smiled and continued, "I would like to show my appreciation. I talked with the elders, and we decided to do something for the village. My business will build a desalination plant. The plant will change salt water to fresh water, so the village will always have fresh water."

Tane and everyone applauded. Tane knew that his family's connection to Tutuila was stronger than ever. He was already looking forward to his next visit!

STOP AND CHECK

How does Tane's attitude about the village change?

video camera

Summarize

Use important details from *Flying Home* to summarize the story. Your graphic organizer may help you.

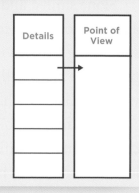

Details	Point of View

Text Evidence

1. How can you tell that *Flying Home* is realistic fiction? Give examples from the text to support your answer. **GENRE**

2. Is this story told by a first-person or third-person narrator? Use details from the story to describe the narrator's point of view. **POINT OF VIEW**

3. On page 13, the author writes "The sunlight danced on the water." What does this mean? How does it add to the story? **PERSONIFICATION**

4. Write about how Tane's meeting with his grandmother would change if it were described by Tane as a first-person narrator. Use details from the story in your answer. **WRITE ABOUT READING**

Compare Texts

Read a poem about how familiy members have a connection through fun and play.

Fun and Play

My Dad says, when he was a boy
He grew up with his brother, Ted, on a farm,
Where he helped my grandma milk the cow
And he kept all the chickens from harm.

He helped his dad chop wood for the fire,
Then stacked the wood in the shed.
And when all of the work was done,
He played baseball in the field with Ted.

Because, rain or shine, there was always time
For outdoor fun and play.

My Mom says, when she was a girl
She lived in a city far away,
Where people scurried like ants
And trains rumbled by every day.

Mom's family lived in a tall, gray block,
They didn't have a lot of space,
But they all worked hard and got along fine,
And her home had a smiling face.

Because, when the work was done, they'd make some time
For indoor fun and play.

My brother and I live in a house
There's a yard with a fence in the back.
And there's Mom and Dad and a shaggy, black dog,
And I don't think there's much that we lack.

Our backyard is a sunny place to play,
Making giant bubbles is a thrill.
We skateboard down the sidewalks to school.
We're not rich, but we're happy still.

Because, when weekends are here, we always find time
For plenty of fun and play.

Make Connections

How do the family members in *Fun and Play* feel connected to the world? **ESSENTIAL QUESTION**

How do the characters in *Flying Home* and "Fun and Play" feel connected to their families? **TEXT TO TEXT**

Focus on
Literary Elements

Imagery in Poetry Poets and other writers use imagery to give readers a stronger sense of the ideas they are writing about. Imagery can include the use of metaphor and simile, or it can simply use vivid, descriptive words. Imagery often uses the five senses (touch, sight, sound, smell, and taste) to help readers form mental images of what is being described.

Read and Find In *Fun and Play*, the narrator uses metaphors, similes, and descriptive language to help the reader visualize the scenes. For example, on page 18 the narrator describes her mom's home as having "a smiling face." Look for other examples of metaphors, similes, and descriptive language in the poem.

Your Turn

With a partner, think of a class or school event, such as a special assembly, a play, or a festival celebration. What could you see, hear, smell, taste, and touch? With your partner, brainstorm words and phrases that describe what you saw, heard, smelled, tasted, and touched. Use the words and phrases to write a short poem about the event. Use at least one example of imagery in the poem. Read the poem aloud to the class.